Activities for **3-5** year olds

All About Us

 Brilliant Publications

Irene Yates

We hope you enjoy using this book. If you would like further information on other titles published by Brilliant Publications, please write to the address given below.

Published by Brilliant Publications, The Old School Yard, Leighton Road, Northall, Dunstable, Bedfordshire LU6 2HA

Written by Irene Yates
Illustrated by Claire Boyce

Printed in Malta by Interprint Limited

© Irene Yates
ISBN 1 897 675 24 0

First published in 1997
10 9 8 7 6 5 4 3 2 1

Contents

Introduction

All About Us looks at the child in her* environment and explores the child's world. The activities are designed to give the child an awareness of herself and her position in society. They have been developed to allow the child to develop consciousness of her own personal attitudes and feelings and to lead to an understanding of the relationship between herself, the people she lives with, and her immediate community.

The activities are organized to work within the framework of SCAA's Desirable Outcomes and take into account the child's developing intellectual, social and physical skills, focusing upon ideas that will encourage the growth of a positive self-image and a positive attitude towards those around her.

Try to adopt a 'play' approach as much as possible, and be flexible. Whatever the focus of any activity, the children will be learning all kinds of things from it and much will depend on your starting point. Always start from what the children already know, and their interests. You should be able to adapt all the activities in this book to work with either individual children or a small group, without too much problem.

The book uses materials which are likely to be readily available within your class or group's location, or which can be easily gathered or collected from the children's families or carers.

All of the activities are designed to give the children confidence and feelings of achievement which, in turn, will become effective tools for learning.

To avoid the clumsy 'he/she', the child is referred to throughout as 'she'.

Learning our names

What children should learn

Language and literacy – to listen and respond, to match name cards to people.

What you need

Paper, crayons, felt-tipped pen, pieces of card.

Activity

Sit the children in a circle. Decide who will be 'on'. Sing, to the tune of 'Ring-a-Roses': 'Somebody's a-knocking, a-knocking at your door. (Child's name, child's name) answer the door.' The child who's on makes up a greeting using the name of a child in the group (eg, 'Hello Sam. Please come in'). This child is the next one to be on. Repeat the song with that child's name. Encourage the children to join in.

Extension

Make a display of the children's self-portraits, with their names written underneath. Print each child's name on a piece of card. As you sing the song, show the name card for the child who is 'on' and point to the letters going from left to right.

Let the children take turns to choose a card, and see if they can work out whose name it is.

Talk about

Who has the same name as someone else? Whose names *begin* with the same sound? Whose names *end* with the same sound?

Recognizing us

What children should learn

Language and literacy – to describe children and begin to recognize some written names.

What you need

Camera or photographs, wall space for display, pieces of card, felt-tipped pen.

Activity

Display a photograph of each child on the wall. Print each child's name on a piece of card (you could use the cards from *Learning our names*, page 5). Work with small groups of children at a time to give them a chance to talk. Read a name card and ask the group which photograph it belongs to. Ask: 'How can we tell it's (child's name)?'. Help them to describe features. Give them the words for blond hair, dark hair, curly hair, straight hair, blue eyes, brown eyes, smiling face, sad face, tall, small, etc.

Extension

Put the name cards face upwards on a surface. Ask the children to find the card which says (child's name). Help them by sounding out the first letter and reminding them what it looks like. Work at this game until they can identify lots of names. Get the children to pick out all the names they know.

Talk about

Why don't we all look the same? Do the children look like their families? How many children have long hair/ short hair? Can we change our faces by smiling/ sulking/frowning, etc?

Guess who I am

What children should learn

Language and literacy – to role play being someone else.

What you need

Dressing up articles, hats, junk materials, paper, felt-tipped pens, crayons.

Activity

Ask four children at a time to think of someone they can pretend to be. Give them some help initially. They may like to be a post person, a bus driver, a doctor, a nurse. The children dress up in clothes of their choice and then stand in front of the rest of the group. They may do a little action to demonstrate their role. The group ask the children questions, in turn, trying to guess who they are. Children who guess correctly first then have a turn.

Extension

Encourage the children to dress up in a role and devise imaginative play together to fit those roles. By joining in the role play yourself you will be able to help the children to develop their roles further. Make junk models that help to reinforce roles, eg walkie talkies for police.

Talk about

Ask the children what it feels like to dress up and pretend to be somebody else. Who would they most like to be? Can they pretend to be someone else and say what that person feels like?

What are we like?

What children should learn

Language and literacy – to increase vocabulary for describing others.

What you need

No special equipment.

Activity

Sit the children in a circle. Choose someone who's not too shy to begin with. Ask the children to look at the child and put up their hand when they can say one positive thing about her. Get them to describe her appearance, what she's wearing, her personality, and the things she likes. Some children will repeat what others have said: that's fine, allow them to verbalize.

Extension

Ask the children to describe themselves. Ask, for example: 'What do you like to do? What's your favourite food?'

Talk about

Try to avoid criticisms. Encourage children to look for, and say, positive things about each other. When has someone shown their friendliness/helped someone else/looked after someone else?

Recording voices

What children should learn

Language and literacy – to talk on a tape recorder and listen and respond to taped instructions.

What you need

A cassette tape recorder.

Activity

Work with small groups. Get the children to make lots of different shapes with their mouths. For example, you could ask them to try to talk through clenched teeth.

Record each child saying something simple, such as their name and how old they are. Replay the tape for them to hear their own voices. Get them to record something else, such as the beginning of a nursery rhyme, without giving their name. The other children listen and decide whose voice it is.

Extension

Record an activity for each child, using their name. For example say, 'Tracey, jump up and down three times; Rashid, nod your head four times; Keeley, shake your hands…' etc. Speak clearly and slowly. Play the tape to the children so that they can respond to 'their' instruction.

Talk about

Do our voices sound the same on tape as off it? Can we make our voices sound different? Who speaks clearly on the tape? How can we do better?

My favourite book

What children should learn

Language and literacy – to listen and respond to stories, and choose their favourite story/book.

What you need

Selection of familiar books.

Activity

This activity can be done with any number of children. Have a session where the children look at books in a quiet way. Give them freedom to share the books with each other and talk about them. Ask if someone could tell the others about a favourite book or story. Encourage the children to be a good, attentive audience whilst individuals stand near to you to speak.

Extension

Make a poster showing each child's favourite story:

Chloe's favourite story is Beauty and the Beast.
Ravinda's favourite story is Where the Wild Things Are.
Jenny's favourite story is Guess How Much I Love You.
Ben's favourite story is Ben's Magic Adventures.

Read the poster out afterwards, pointing to the children's names and the titles so that the children can join in.

Talk about

General discussion of books and stories is always good language practice. Ask what books they like. Why? Who reads to them? Which stories can they remember best? Can anyone tell a story to the group?

What sizes are we?

What children should learn

Mathematics – to compare sizes.

What you need

Mirror, large sheet of paper, felt-tipped pen, Blu-tack, playdough.

Activity

Work with a small group of children. Help the children to compare their sizes. Who is tallest? Who is shortest? Compare their sizes with those of adult carers. Fasten a large sheet of paper to the wall. Measure and mark the height of the children on the paper. Get them to make themselves taller and shorter by standing on tiptoe or curling up. Compare the children stretching their arms out – who can stretch the widest?

Extension

Compare objects in the room. Who can touch the top of the bookcase/playhouse/slide, etc? How many children holding hands in a chain does it take to measure the width of the window/the table/the door, etc? Who can curl up into the smallest ball?

Talk about

Use comparison words. Can they make a snake out of playdough that is *longer* than their hand? Can they make one that is *shorter*? How can the children measure small objects using their hands and fingers? How many hands wide is the book? How many hands tall is the play car? Teach the following rhyme and make up rhymes to go with it:

As tall as a house
As small as a mouse
As wide as a bridge
As thin as a pin.

Measuring hands and feet

What children should learn

Mathematics – to develop an understanding of size.

What you need

Paper, felt-tipped pen, scissors.

Activity

Work with a small group of children. Get them to stand on a sheet of paper and draw round their feet. Cut each child's 'feet' out separately and write their names on each foot clearly. Make a line of pairs of feet along the floor, then get the children to put them in order, starting with either the longest or the shortest. Do the same activity drawing round hands instead of feet.

Extension

Get the children to measure the room, or a smaller space, by placing one foot in front of the other and counting their footsteps. Is it the same number of footsteps for each child? Why are there differences? Get the children to draw and colour their socks. Mix up the feet and then match the pairs.

Talk about

Why aren't everyone's hands and feet the same size? Are their feet the same size as each other? Are their hands? Can they find someone who has smaller/bigger hands than them?

Sam   Ahmed   Jane

Sam   Ahmed   Jane   Mrs Brown

How many children?

What children should learn

Mathematics – to develop counting skills.

What you need

A cassette player, music.

Activity

Work with five or six children. Count all the children in the group, out loud, getting them to join in where they can. Put the music on for dancing. Stop the music and say: 'All the children wearing red shoes sit down'. Count the children who are still standing. Play the music again. When you stop it, get another set of children to sit down, and so on until there is no one left to dance.

Extension

Count the children in groups, eg having drinks or drawing. How many children are there? Count again, starting with a different child each time. Is the total still the same?

Talk about

Ask the children whether there are more children in one group than another, the same, or less. Use constant reinforcement to get them to use the words and understand the concepts.

How far?

What children should learn

Mathematics – to gain some understanding of measuring a space.

What you need

Space, bean bags, chalk, paper, crayons, felt-tipped pen.

Activity

Have all the children sitting in a row. Ask them to take turns to see how far they can jump or hop in one go and how far they can throw a bean bag. Use the chalk to mark where the bean bag throw lands. Get them to measure the distance of their bean bag throw in jumps and hops. (Note: tiptoe fairy steps could be used if a child cannot yet hop.) If it takes more hops than jumps, does this mean the size of the space changes?

Extension

Work on 'how far' by getting the children to record their hops or jumps. Prepare a simple record sheet for each child. The children could draw a picture of the beanbag. Help them to write their name and the number of hops they did.

Talk about

Use phrases such as 'how far', 'how near', 'who is closest to', 'which is the furthest away', 'which is the closest' to discuss the activity.

Priya threw a beanbag. It took 5 hops to reach it.

Behind/in front of

What children should learn

Mathematics – to use maths language to describe position.

What you need

Large, clear space.

Activity

Work with a group of six to eight children. They should be used to playing 'follow the leader'. Have them all sitting on the floor to begin with then call out one child to stand up. Call the other children to stand up, one at a time, telling them to stand either 'in front of' or 'behind' one of the children already standing. Continue until all the children are in line, then let the leader make a pathway to be followed. Play the game often so that all the children have a chance to be leader.

Extension

You can make this game harder by instructing children to be 'two in front of' or 'four behind', etc.

Talk about

Discuss the other language you might use for positioning in this way, eg 'before' and 'after' and get the children to listen carefully for your instructions. Use the words 'first', 'second', 'third', etc and 'last'. Some children may also be able to understand 'last but one'.

Tallest/shortest

What children should learn

Mathematics – to use mathematical language to compare size.

What you need

Long strips of paper (about 15 cm wide), chalk, felt-tipped pen, large building blocks.

Activity

Work with small groups of children. Let the children lie down, one at a time, with their feet against a wall or solid object. Cut a strip of paper so that it is the same height as the child. Write the children's names on their strips. Encourage the children to compare their strips and decide who is the tallest, who is the shortest. Ask: 'Are any children exactly the same height?'. The children could line up blocks on their strip and count how many blocks it takes.

Extension

Compare the children's strips to the size of an adult. Use a mirror to help them compare heights. Measure the heights of the children on an outside wall and let the children draw a line in chalk to show how tall they are.

Talk about

Use the words 'height', 'taller than', 'shorter than', 'tallest', 'shortest'. Ask who can reach 'highest', who can reach 'lowest'.

Our friends are ...

What children should learn

Personal and social development – to show an awareness of others around them.

What you need

Paper, crayons.

Activity

Use a tune the children know well, or make up a little tune, to sing the words: 'We're all friends together, together, together. We're all friends together – yes we are.' Choose a child to sing the next bit. The child chooses a 'friend' and sings the name, eg 'Sophie is my friend, my friend, my friend. Sophie is my friend – all day long.' The next step is to ask Sophie how she will be a friend to the first child today. Sophie then sings the next verse, choosing someone else, and so on, round the group.

Extension

Have the children draw pictures of their friends. Help them to write their own names and their friends' names.

Talk about

Get the children to discuss what's good about friends, how they can be a good friend and how they can play well together.

Exploring feelings

What children should learn

Personal and social development – to develop sensitivity to others' feelings and to express their own feelings.

What you need

Magazines, scissors, paper, glue.

Activity

Work with a group of four or five children. Play a mime game where the children copy miming happy faces/ sad faces/frowning/laughing/scowling faces, etc. Ask the children to describe what people are feeling when they make such faces.

Help the children to cut faces from the magazines and describe whether they are sad, happy, etc. Stick each child's picture to a sheet of paper.

Extension

Bring the pictures back to the group and ask the children to decide what might have happened to make the faces happy, sad, etc.

Talk about

Discuss the things that make people/children happy and the things that make them sad. How do they feel when they are sick or hurt themselves? How do they feel when they are going to do something exciting?

What do we wear?

What children should learn

Personal and social development – to manipulate different types of fasteners in order to dress themselves.

What you need

Lots of items of clothing for dressing up, with a variety of fasteners.

Activity

You can do this activity with any size group. Show the children all the different fasteners. Do they know what all the fasteners are called? Look for zips, buttons, velcro, laces, buckles, press studs, hooks and eyes. Help the children to manipulate the various fasteners.

Extension

Mime the actions of getting up in the morning, washing, dressing, getting ready to leave the home. Encourage the children to help each other into the dressing up clothes, doing up the fasteners, etc.

Talk about

How do we know which way our clothes go on? How can we tell the fronts from the backs? How do we know which is the right shoe for each foot?

Keeping safe

What children should learn

Personal and social development – to develop an understanding that traffic can be dangerous and that we need to take care in crossing the road.

What you need

Masking tape, cardboard 'lollipop' for lollipop person.

Activity

Work with a group of four or five children. Talk to the group about how they keep safe in the street. Help them to make a simple plan of the roads outside the school or playgroup by marking the floor with masking tape. Explain the rules of crossing safely. Divide the group into children, lollipop person and traffic. Play 'crossing the road'. Let the children take turns at the different roles.

Extension

Bring the children together in the group and ask them to describe their parts in the activity. Did they all cross safely? If they were 'traffic' did they slow down and watch for children crossing?

Talk about

Make sure the children understand that crossing with a lollipop person at a crossing is not a guarantee of safety and they still have to be vigilant.

Caring for someone else

What children should learn

Personal and social development – to be sensitive to the needs and feelings of others.

What you need

Home corner resources, dolls, dolls' clothes.

Activity

Work with a group of four or five children. Help the children to set up a baby corner with the home corner resources. What do they need to look after a baby? How can they keep the baby happy? What makes babies unhappy? Encourage the children to play at looking after the baby, stressing gentleness, quietness and safety.

Extension

Invite a mother and baby into the group and ask the mother to talk to the children about her role in looking after the baby. Provide dolls and dolls' clothes for the children to act out their caring role.

Talk about

Who else could need looking after? How can the children ensure that they always act in a caring way? Do they care for one another? How? Who cares for them? How do they care for themselves?

I can follow

What children should learn

Personal and social development – to work confidently as part of the group.

What you need

Space.

Activity

This activity can be done with any number of children. This is a 'follow the leader' activity which gives the children understanding of taking turns, following and being the leader. Lead the line yourself at first. Make a clear pathway in the space with the children in line behind you. You might march in straight lines, hop in zigzag lines, run or skip in curved, twisting lines, tiptoe in lines that change direction, etc.

Extension

Give the children plenty of encouragement and opportunities to take turns as the leader. Let them decide how to move and what kind of direction the line will take, so that they all have a chance to follow and to lead.

Talk about

Ask the children: 'What different ways could we move? Could we be higher or lower? How? Could we go in a different direction? What does it feel like to follow? What does it feel like to be the leader?'

A picture of me

What children should learn

Creative development – to make choices about colour, shape, space and texture while making a life-size picture of themselves.

What you need

Large sheets of paper (eg wallpaper), adhesive tape, felt-tipped pen, crayons or paints, glue, odds and ends of fabric, wool, mirrors, etc.

Activity

Tape together sheets of paper, if necessary. Get the children to lie down, in turn, on the sheet of paper and draw round their outline. Encourage the children to name body parts as you draw. Cut out each 'child'. Ask the children what kind of clothes they'd like to stick on their shape. Would they like the clothes they are wearing today, or something else? Help the children to colour in and stick fabrics and odds and ends to their shape.

Extension

Use the mirror to help the children confirm their ideas about their own appearance. If you have a second mirror use it to show the children a back view of themselves. Use the pictures for a large display.

Talk about

Help the children to remember the names of different body parts. Encourage them to describe themselves and others in words, eg eyes and hair colours, clothing. Talk with the children about the choices they make. For example: 'What colour fabric would you like? Is this piece big enough? What are you going to put on your feet?'

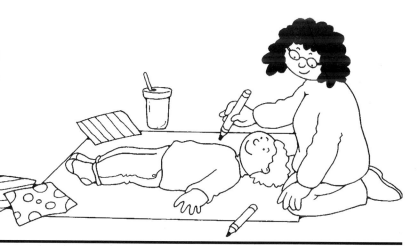

I can dance

What children should learn

Creative development – to listen and respond imaginatively to music.

What you need

A tape or disc player, some soft flowing music and some rhythmic music (taped before the session), crayons or paint, paper.

Activity

This activity can be done with any number of children. Sit the children in a space to listen to the first piece of music. Ask them to close their eyes and just listen. What kind of feeling does the music give them? Play the music again and ask the children to listen carefully and dance the feeling that the music gives them. Repeat with a different kind of music.

Extension

Get the children to paint or crayon to the same pieces of music. They should be listening as they are doing the task so that their artwork is a response to the music.

Talk about

Ask them which kind of music they like best – gentle, peaceful, warm – or fast, rhythmic, heavy beat music? Can they dance to all kinds of music? Can they describe the music they like?

I can listen

What children should learn

Creative development – to respond to sounds.

What you need

A collection of instruments – tambourines, castanets, sticks, chime bars, rattles, bells.

Activity

This activity can be done with any number of children. Teach the children to make a different response to two or three instruments, eg jump in the air when they see and hear the rattle; clap their hands when they see and hear the tambourine; sit down when they see and hear the castanets, etc. Add more sounds and responses as their confidence develops.

Extension

When the children are really confident play the instruments behind a screen so that they can't see them. Ask them to respond to the sound.

Talk about

Talk about what different movements they could make for each instrument. Let them decide all together and take turns making the sounds.

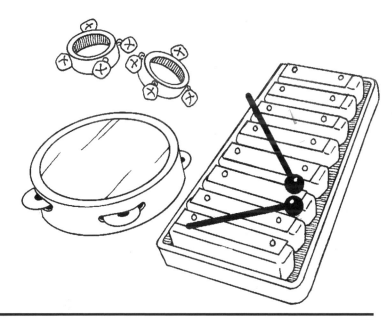

Look at me!

What children should learn

Physical development – to move confidently with increasing control and awareness.

What you need

Large, clear space.

Activity

This activity can be done with any number of children. Ask the children what would happen if the floor surface all of a sudden changed. Ask them to respond imaginatively with different kinds of movements. Suggest a wet, puddly floor; a sticky, muddy floor; a slippery, slidy floor; a hot, on-fire floor; a jagged, rocky floor; a wet, sinking floor, etc.

Extension

Ask different children to demonstrate their response to the change you have suggested and get the other children to imitate their actions.

Talk about

Talk about the responses the children make. Do they bounce, leap, jump, step, balance, run, hop, reach, stretch, clamber, stamp, sink, pull, stretch? Give them the words for their actions by saying, for example: 'Oh (child's name) is doing some good bouncing over there', etc.

Let's move

What children should learn

Physical development – to move confidently and imaginatively.

What you need

Large, clear space.

Activity

Work with the whole group. Ask the children to think of ways of moving using their feet; using their hands and feet; using no hands or feet. Ask them to think of ways of moving which use crawling, creeping, wriggling, sliding, rolling. Ask the children to sit as still as possible between each movement (give a fun signal, such as a hand wiggle or a finger click, when you want them to start or stop).

Extension

Get individual children to demonstrate their movements to the group and let the group copy them. Make a pattern of three or four movements with stillness in between them and ask the children to follow it.

Talk about

What movements can they do:
- on their feet?
- on their hands and feet?
- on their tummies?
- on their bottoms?
- on their knees?

What other parts of the body move? Talk about tongues, jaws, toes, lips, eyelids, etc.

Two little hands

What children should learn

Physical development – to make patterns of movements with their hands.

What you need

No special equipment.

Activity

Work with a small group of children. Ask the children to hold up two hands and count 'one, two'. Get them to lower one hand and count their fingers and thumb on the remaining hand, 'one, two, three, four, five'. Raise other hand again and practise counting to ten.

With two hands they can make counting patterns in the air. For example: one clap, two claps, one wave, two waves, etc. Make up a short repeating pattern using:

claps

waves

fists

roll overs

For example, one wave, two fists, three claps, four roll overs. Count with the children as you repeat the pattern together.

Extension

Work up to the point where the children can remember a short pattern and count it out in their heads instead of aloud.

Talk about

Examine and discuss hands. Name all the basic parts and talk about what they're for, ie nails, knuckles, etc. Compare soft and hard parts of the hands. Make up a song or rhyme doing lots of different actions with the hands and fingers. For instance: 'Two little hands go clap, clap, clap. Four little fingers go tap, tap, tap. Two little thumbs go wiggle, wiggle, wiggle. Two little wrists go wriggle, wriggle, wriggle.'

Naming our body parts

What children should learn

Knowledge and understanding of the world – to name specific parts of the body, thus increasing vocabulary.

What you need

Lots of space, dolls, teddies, etc.

Activity

Work with small groups. Make sure each child has a toy with body parts. You can play this game using whichever words the children need to be familiarized with. For example, some children may be at the stage of naming head, arms and legs, whilst others may be up to elbows, fingertips, ankles, etc.

Ask the child to look at her toy. Ask: 'Has it got a head/eyes/elbows, etc? Show me where they are. Show me your head/eyes/elbows.' Let the children take turns to suggest parts of the body. If they don't know the names give them the word clearly then repeat it. Get them to repeat it back to you. Repeat it again to them, then look for the part on the toy.

Extension

Add more parts and more vocabulary as the children learn. Teach them the song 'Hands, shoulders, knees and toes'. Encourage the children to touch the relevant part of their body as they sing. The tune can start off slowly, but gradually get faster so that the children are touching the body parts quickly and almost curling up by the time they get to 'knees and toes' and the repeat of 'knees and toes'.

Talk about

Say: 'Show me your head/eyes/elbows'. Ask: 'What's this part called?', or 'Where's my elbow/knee/ankle?', etc.

Lots of faces

What children should learn

Knowledge and understanding of the world – to explore different expressions and actions.

What you need

Mirrors.

Activity

Work with three or four children. Get the children to look into the mirrors and name the parts of their faces. Have the children pull faces at themselves and mimic the faces pulled at each other. Mime face actions (crying/sneezing/laughing, etc) and ask the children to name what you are doing and copy the action.

Extension

Get the children to close their eyes and follow instructions. For example: 'Put your hand on your chin/tap your nose/scratch your ears/put a finger on your forehead', etc.

Talk about

How many eyes do they have? How many ears? How many noses? Chins? Foreheads? Cheeks? Lips? Where are their teeth? Where are their ears? Get them to answer in words, not just by touching and indicating.

Who do we live with?

What children should learn

Knowledge and understanding of the world – to listen to others and talk about their own lives.

What you need

Magazine pictures of adults and children who could be mothers, fathers, brothers, sisters, grandparents, aunts, uncles, babies.

Activity

Talk about the people who might live all together in one home, and get the children to discuss who lives at their home. Explain, simply, the relationships between sisters, brothers, parents, grandparents and themselves. Show the children the magazine pictures and get them to make up a 'family group' with them. Stick the pictures to a sheet of paper and get the children to name the characters.

Extension

With the children, make up a story about a family. Decide who is in the family, where they live, and what their daily routines are. Let the children make up and cut out a 'family' of their own from a magazine.

Talk about

Discuss the fact that we all have different kinds of families. Try to use as many of the 'relations' words as you can. Keep your explanations simple.

My own puppet

What children should learn

Knowledge and understanding of the world – to explore and select materials and use skills for puppet making.

What you need

Paper plates, adhesive tape, strong card, sticky paper, wool, sequins, bits of fabric, scissors, elastic band.

Activity

Work with five or six children. Explain to the group that they are going to make a puppet of someone in their family, or a friend. Help them to decide who their puppet will be. Use the paper plates for heads. Encourage the children to sort through the materials to find appropriate pieces. While the children are sorting, talk about the textures of the materials. Are they heavy or light? Can they feel the patterns or only see them? What kind of material would be good for hair? Are some materials easier to cut than others? Help them to stick their chosen materials to the plate. When the head is done to their satisfaction, tape a strip of strong card to the back so that they can hold their puppet.

Extension

Scraps of fabric tied at the top with elastic bands make good disguises for little hands and arms. Get the children to organize their puppets 'talking to each other'.

Talk about

Ask the children: 'What kind of hair does your puppet need? What colour eyes? How shall we do the nose? Is the mouth a smiling mouth', etc?

scrap of fabric

elastic band

adhesive tape

strip of strong card

front   back